KING IN TRAINING:

GODLY WISDOM FOR MY YOUNGER SELF

LESSONS ON MANHOOD, INTEGRITY, & FAITH

ROBERT P. HARRIS, JR.

King In Training: Godly Wisdom For My Younger Self

Robert P. Harris, Jr.

Copyright @ 2025 Robert P. Harris, Jr. All rights reserved.

King In Training: Godly Wisdom For My Younger Self

Robert P. Harris, Jr.

LESSONS ON MANHOOD, INTREGRITY, & FAITH

DEDICATION

I dedicate this book to my loving wife, Tiffany Harris. Thank you for your unwavering support, encouragement, and for continually pushing me to see this project through to the end. Your belief in me made all the difference.

I also dedicate this work to my amazing children, Robert I. Harris and Moriah E. Harris. You inspire me every day to be a better man, a stronger father, and a faithful example. This book is for you.

Robert P. Harris, Jr.

King In Training: Godly Wisdom For My Younger Self

Robert P. Harris, Jr.

CHAPTER 1:

CROWNING BEGINS AT THE CROSS

UNDERSTANDING IDENTITY, PURPOSE, AND SUBMISSION TO GOD AS THE FOUNDATION OF MANHOOD

Manhood is not something you stumble into—it is something you grow into. And the first step of that growth begins not on a throne, but at the foot of the cross.

Before a man can lead, he must learn to follow. Before he can rule, he must learn to serve. Before he can walk in confidence, he must learn humility. These lessons are not learned in the world's classroom, but in the presence of God. For the crown of true manhood begins with submission to the will of God.

My Beginning

For me, this journey began with a woman of quiet strength—my grandmother, the late **Bertha Marion**. She introduced me to Jesus Christ before I even fully understood who I was. She made sure I went to church, recited the **Lord's Prayer**, and knew how to reverence the things of God. I didn't realize it then, but she was laying down the bricks of spiritual discipline that would become the road I walked as a man.

She sowed seeds of faith, prayer, and reverence into my young life. Her Bible stayed worn, her words were full of wisdom, and her prayers covered me. She believed in a God who transforms boys into men of valor—and I was the beneficiary of her prayers.

A Place to Grow: The Royal Rangers

At **Community Chapel Assembly of God** in **Shelby, Mississippi,** I found more than a church— I found a safe space to grow. A Christian boys' program called **Royal Rangers** became a critical part of my foundation. Led by a compassionate and patient man named **Mr. Prince,** the Royal Rangers taught us about life from a biblical perspective. They instilled values in us that were quickly fading from society.

I learned things like:
- **How to pray and understand salvation**
- **What it means to honor your word**
- **How to show respect for elders and authority**
- **Why character matters even when no one is watching**
- **How to live with purpose, guided by God's Word**

We practiced tying knots, earning badges, and reciting scriptures, but it was deeper than that—it was formation. Royal Rangers was more than a program. It was preparation for life. Mr. Prince didn't just care that we showed up. He cared that we grew up—into godly men who would take responsibility, honor God, and lead with conviction.

Those early years taught me that my masculinity didn't need to be loud to be powerful. It needed to be rooted in truth, compassion, and godliness. It was okay to cry in God's presence. It was honorable to serve others. It was noble to walk in integrity when no one else was.

CROWNED AT THE CROSS

When I look back, I realize that everything I am becoming started with those early moments— kneeling in prayer, singing in the pews, learning memory verses, wearing the Royal Rangers uniform with pride. But the real uniform of a godly man isn't made of fabric. It's made of **faith, humility, and purpose**.

You cannot wear the **crown of manhood** until you've picked up the **cross of Christ**.

And that crown? It doesn't shine because of status or success. It shines because it's been refined by surrender—surrender to the One who knows who you are and why you were created.

REFLECTION QUESTIONS

1. Who introduced you to your first understanding of God? How did their influence shape your life?
2. In what ways are you still discovering your identity in Christ?
3. What does it mean to you personally to take up your cross and follow Jesus as a man?
4. How can surrendering to God's will be a strength rather than a weakness?
5. What values or disciplines from your youth are helping (or could help) you grow into godly manhood today?

Personal Prayer

Heavenly Father,

Thank You for the cross that reveals my identity and purpose. Thank You for the people You placed in my life—like my grandmother—who helped point me toward You. Help me to never forget that real manhood begins with surrender, not self-promotion. Teach me to walk in humility, to serve with honor, and to lead with love. May I always look to You before I look to the world. In Jesus' name, *Amen.*

KINGLY CHALLENGES

- **Honor Your Foundation:**
  Take a moment this week to thank someone who helped introduce you to Christ. Call them, write a letter, or share their legacy with someone else.

- **Memorize Your Identity:**
  Commit **Galatians 2:20** to memory. Let it become the foundation of how you see yourself every day.

- **Start a "Manhood Journal":**
  Write one paragraph about who you want to become as a man of God. Be honest. Be bold. Let this journal become your personal road map.

- **Serve in Silence:**
  Do one act of service this week without expecting praise—just like Jesus served us. This could be helping at home, assisting someone in need, or simply listening.

Robert P. Harris, Jr.

Chapter 2:
Stand Firm

BUILDING UNSHAKABLE INTEGRITY AND MORAL COURAGE IN A WORLD THAT TESTS YOUR VALUES

The world we live in today often blurs the line between right and wrong. Men are praised for popularity, wealth, or dominance—but rarely for integrity. Yet, integrity is what sets a godly man apart. It is the inner strength to do what is right even when no one is watching, even when it costs you, even when it's hard.

Integrity is not just about big decisions; it's built in the small, daily choices—telling the truth, keeping your word, resisting temptation, and standing firm in your convictions. A man without values is like a building with no foundation—easily shaken and quickly destroyed. But a man who stands on God's truth is unshakable.

Moral courage is the bravery to do what honors God even when others mock, question, or abandon you for it. Remember, even Jesus stood alone at times. But He stood firm—so that you would have the power to do the same.

Godly men are rare, not because it's impossible, but because it's uncomfortable. It takes strength to walk away from gossip, to refuse to cheat, to honor women, to confess your mistakes, and to choose prayer over pride. But each of those choices chisels your character and makes you a true king in training.

When you live by your values, not your feelings, your foundation becomes solid. Feelings change with the wind, but values anchored in Christ will hold firm through any storm.

I played football from grade school to post-college. The game of football taught me many lessons that still apply to everyday life. On the field, you quickly learn the results of both good and bad decisions. A missed block, a late hit, or a poor attitude can cost your team valuable yardage. In life, the same is true—our decisions can move us forward or set us back.

In football, the goal is always forward progress. That should be a life goal, too. We will all experience setbacks—injuries, mistakes, missed plays. But just like in football, how we respond matters. Having **integrity**, **good morals**, and **strong character** will help us bounce back from life's hardest hits. The scoreboard isn't always the final say—your faith and fortitude are.

You may feel pressure to fit in, to compromise, or to remain silent. But God doesn't need silent men—He needs courageous ones. Stand firm when others fold. Speak truth when others lie. Be faithful when others drift. Live boldly, knowing that your strength comes not from applause, but from the One who called you.

You don't have to follow the crowd to be a man. Stand firm. Let your character speak louder than your clothes. Let your heart be known by heaven, not hyped by culture. When you stand firm in Christ, you're never standing alone.

Reflection Questions

1. When was the last time your integrity was tested? How did you respond?
2. What are three core values you want to define your manhood?
3. How can you build moral courage even when you're afraid of standing alone?
4. What does it mean to you to "stand firm" in God's Word?
5. Can you recall a time in sports or life when you had to bounce back? What helped you?

Personal Prayer

Lord God,

Make me a man who stands firm in truth. Teach me to value integrity more than approval. Give me the courage to do what's right, even when it's not popular. Help me to be faithful in small things so You can trust me with greater things. Let my life reflect Your light in a dark world. When I fall short or get knocked down, remind me that with You, I can get back up and move forward. In Jesus' name, *Amen.*

Kingly Challenges

- **List Your Values:**
  Write down five godly values you want to live by. Post them where you'll see them daily.

- **Practice Integrity:**
  This week, follow through on every commitment—big or small—even if no one notices.

- **Encourage Courage:**
  Stand up for someone who is being mistreated, left out, or overlooked. Be a voice for what's right.

- **Reflect Like a Player:**
  Think about a mistake you made recently—on or off the "field." What lesson did God show you through it? Journal your bounce-back strategy.

Chapter 3:
Guard Your Heart, Rule Your Mind

WISDOM FOR EMOTIONAL STRENGTH, SELF-CONTROL, AND SPIRITUAL RESILIENCE

One of the greatest battles you'll ever face as a man isn't on a field or in a courtroom—it's in your own heart and mind. Proverbs 4:23 tells us, *"Above all else, guard your heart, for everything you do flows from it."* Your heart is your spiritual command center. Whatever you allow into it—whether good or bad—will shape your actions, choices, relationships, and destiny.

I knew a young man growing up who had all the athletic talent in the world. Fast, strong, and gifted—everyone said he was going to "go pro" one day. Coaches loved him. Scouts watched him. He had everything he needed physically to succeed. But he didn't guard his heart or rule his mind.

He got caught up in the wrong crowd—people who didn't care about his future, only his attention. He started experimenting with drugs, alcohol, and skipping class. At first, it seemed harmless, just a little fun. But slowly, his discipline disappeared. His work ethic faded. His grades dropped. He got suspended from the team, and eventually, he dropped out of school altogether.

That young man never made it to the pros. He had the talent, but he didn't have the character. He had potential, but no self-control. He could play the game, but he couldn't win the battle inside his own soul.

As men of God, we must take this seriously. The enemy is not only after your body—he's after your heart and mind. He uses anger, addiction, lust, pride, and fear as weapons to destroy your focus and pull you away from your purpose. The moment you stop guarding your heart is the moment you give the enemy access to your future.

Guarding your heart doesn't mean living in fear. It means living with **wisdom**. It means setting boundaries, choosing godly friends, praying daily, and filtering what you watch, hear, and say. It means staying away from substances and people who bring out the worst in you.

Ruling your mind means taking your thoughts captive (2 Corinthians 10:5). You can't stop negative thoughts from showing up—but you don't have to invite them in for dinner. Feed your mind the Word of God. Fill your thoughts with things that are *true, noble, pure, and praiseworthy* (Philippians 4:8). A strong mind builds an unshakable man.

You're not weak because you struggle. You're weak when you ignore the struggle and allow it to rule you. But with the power of God, you can overcome every temptation and walk in purity, power, and purpose.

Never forget: **the real victory starts in your heart.**

Reflection Questions

1. What negative influences are you currently allowing into your heart or mind?
2. How do you respond when you feel tempted, angry, or discouraged?
3. What healthy boundaries do you need to set to protect your heart and mind?
4. Are your current habits drawing you closer to God—or further away?

PERSONAL PRAYER

Lord,

I ask for Your help in guarding my heart and ruling my mind. Teach me how to walk in wisdom, avoid temptation, and stay focused on the calling You have placed on my life. Remove any thoughts, habits, or people that are pulling me away from You. Replace them with truth, discipline, and peace. Strengthen me to live with emotional maturity and spiritual resilience. I want to honor You in every area of my life. In Jesus' name, *Amen.*

KINGLY CHALLENGES

- **Clean Your Inner Circle:**
  Evaluate your friendships. Are they helping or hurting your walk with God? Cut ties with those leading you toward destruction.

- **Set a Guard:**
  Identify one area where you've been letting your guard down—social media, music, relationships, or substances—and make a new boundary this week.

- **Feed Your Mind:**
  Read or memorize **Philippians 4:8** and begin your day by thinking on what is *pure, excellent, and worthy of praise*.

- **Start a Heart Journal:**
  Each night this week, write down what affected your heart the most that day—good or bad. Reflect and pray over it.

King In Training: Godly Wisdom For My Younger Self

Chapter 4:

Work Like a King-in-Waiting

Developing a Strong Work Ethic, Discipline, and Responsibility as Acts of Worship

A king-in-waiting doesn't waste time—he prepares, trains, and builds. He understands that before you wear the crown, you must learn to carry the weight of responsibility. That journey begins with work.

Work is not a curse—it is a calling. From the beginning, God gave Adam responsibility in the garden before He gave him a title or a partner. Work teaches us **discipline**, **dignity**, and **devotion**. When done with the right heart, work becomes an act of worship.

My great-grandfather, **Mr. John Robert Harris**, laid the foundation for my family with his hands, his wisdom, and his unwavering faith. Though I never met him, I feel like I know him deeply. His legacy didn't die with him, it lived on through his sons, who became my uncles, and through my father. Each one of them carried a piece of his excellence and passed it down to me.

He taught his sons valuable trades: **carpentry, brick masonry, contracting, auto mechanics, farming, music, and ministry**. These weren't just jobs, they were tools for life. They gave our family the ability to create, to provide, and to contribute meaningfully to the world around us. From fixing engines to building homes, from harvesting crops to leading worship, the spirit of work flowed like an inheritance.

As I watched my father and uncles work with their hands, I was learning more than skills. I was learning honor. I was learning the joy of completing a task, the discipline of rising early, the humility of doing a job well even if no one noticed. It's amazing to think that a man I never met could shape my life so deeply—but that's the power of legacy built on godly labor.

In today's culture, many people avoid hard work and chase shortcuts. But there's no shortcut to greatness. Kings aren't born in palaces; they're forged in fields, workshops, classrooms, and early mornings. Before David sat on the throne, he shepherded sheep. Before Joseph ruled Egypt, he served in prison. Their rise to royalty was marked by responsibility, not entitlement.

A king-in-waiting shows up early, honors commitments, learns from correction, and takes pride in doing things with excellence. He doesn't work just for a paycheck—he works to glorify God.

Colossians 3:23 says, *"Whatever you do, work heartily, as for the Lord and not for men."* That includes your job, your schoolwork, your chores, your ministry, and your dreams. When you work like you're working for God, everything becomes holy.

You may not have a throne right now, but you have a field. You have a responsibility. You have an assignment. Work with excellence. Prepare like you're being watched by the King of kings— because you are.

Every time you swing a hammer, take notes in class, mow a lawn, help your family, or lead a team—you are practicing kingship. Let your work ethic speak before your words ever do. A king-in-waiting never forgets **how you work while waiting prepares you for what you're working toward.**

REFLECTION QUESTIONS

1. What skills or values have been passed down to you from your family legacy?
2. How do you view work—as a burden or as an opportunity to worship?
3. What areas of your life need more discipline or excellence right now?
4. Are there ways you can honor your family's legacy by working with greater purpose?

Personal Prayer

Heavenly Father,

Thank You for the legacy of godly labor that has been passed down to me. Teach me to value work, not as punishment, but as worship. Help me build discipline, responsibility, and perseverance. Let my hands reflect Your excellence and my heart reflect Your humility. I may not have a crown yet but help me work like a king-in-waiting—faithful, focused, and fearless. In Jesus' name, *Amen.*

Kingly Challenges

- **Learn a Legacy Skill:**
  Choose one skill (carpentry, budgeting, fixing things, or music) passed down in your family and start practicing it weekly.
- **Serve with Excellence:**
  Pick a task you usually rush through—this time, do it with full focus and excellence as an offering to God.
- **Reflect and Record:**
  Write a journal entry about how your work habits reflect your spiritual maturity. Set one goal for improvement this week.
- **Honor a Hard Worker:**
  Thank or honor someone in your life who modeled a strong work ethic—your parent, grandparent, coach, or teacher. Tell them how it impacted you.

Robert P. Harris, Jr.

Chapter 5:
Respect Is Royalty

LEARNING TO HONOR WOMEN, ELDERS, YOURSELF, AND OTHERS THROUGH GODLY RESPECT

Respect isn't just good manners, it's a mindset, a lifestyle, and a sign of true leadership. In God's kingdom, respect is not optional. It is essential. A young man may grow in strength, skill, and popularity, but if he lacks respect, he forfeits the crown God wants to place on his life. Respect is what separates a foolish boy from a wise king-in-training.

One of the greatest blessings in my life was being raised by a strong, wise mother and two Godfearing grandmothers. These women didn't just teach me how to act—they taught me how to *honor*. My grandmothers walked in grace and strength and commanded respect without saying a word. My mother was more direct. She looked me in the eye one day and said, "Robert, never treat a woman in a way that you wouldn't want someone treating me, your grandmothers, or your sister." That truth hit me deep—and it stayed with me.

From them, I learned that true manhood isn't proven by force or dominance, but by how you treat the women around you. If I could love and protect the women in my family, then I had no excuse not to show that same level of honor to every woman I encountered. God expects us to reflect His love, not just in public but in private, in our thoughts, words, and actions.

1 Peter 3:7 (NIV) says, *"Husbands, in the same way be considerate as you live with your wives and treat them with respect... so that nothing will hinder your prayers."* That scripture taught me that how I treat women even affects my relationship with God. Disrespect can block your blessings.

But respect goes beyond women—it starts with how you treat **yourself**. A king who doesn't respect himself will fall for anything. When you know who you are in God, you walk with confidence and discipline. You don't need to curse for attention, fight for validation, or follow the crowd to feel important. Self-respect means knowing your worth and setting standards that honor your future.

1 Corinthians 10:31 reminds us, *"So whether you eat or drink or whatever you do, do it all for the glory of God."* This includes how you dress, how you speak, how you respond to pressure, and how you treat your own body. You glorify God when you live with self-control.

Another powerful lesson I learned growing up was to **respect my elders and those in authority**. My mother, grandmothers, and community leaders made sure I understood that being younger did not give me the right to be disrespectful. I was taught to listen to those who came before me, to speak when spoken to, and to honor the wisdom that comes with age and experience.

Even when I didn't agree or fully understand, I was taught to respond with humility. That kind of respect has opened more doors for me than any talent ever could. **Proverbs 1:8-9 (NIV)** says, *"Listen, my son, to your father's instruction and do not forsake your mother's teaching. They are a garland to grace your head and a chain to adorn your neck."*

Respect for authority also means honoring coaches, teachers, law enforcement, and spiritual leaders. God places authority figures in our lives for a reason—even if we don't always understand it. **Romans 13:1 (NLT)** says, *"Everyone must submit to governing authorities. For all authority comes from God, and those in positions of authority have been placed there by God."*

Respect is also required in how we treat our **peers and strangers**. Whether it's your classmates, teammates, or someone you just met, everyone deserves to be treated with dignity. **Luke 6:31** gives us a timeless principle: *"Do to others as you would have them do to you."*

Here's the truth: being respectful can take you farther than you ever imagined. It will cause people to speak well of you in rooms you've never walked into. Coaches will trust you. Employers will recommend you. Mentors will invest in you. Opportunities will come your way not just because of what you can do, but because of how you treat people. Respect draws favor. It creates a reputation of reliability, integrity, and strength—and that's what true kings are made of.

Every king must learn that respect is not weakness—it's a sign of maturity, wisdom, and character. When you walk in respect, you reflect the heart of God and prepare yourself for real leadership.

REFLECTION QUESTIONS

1. How were you taught to show respect growing up?
2. Why do you think respecting authority is important for a young man becoming a king in training?
3. What are some ways you can show respect to elders, parents, and teachers in your daily life?
4. How does honoring others reflect your relationship with God?
5. Think of someone you respect deeply — what qualities do they have that earn your respect?

PERSONAL PRAYER

Father God, thank You for the powerful women in my life who taught me what it means to show love, protection, and respect. Thank You for my mother and both of my grandmothers, who set the standard and gave me a foundation of honor. Thank You for those who taught me to value my elders and respect authority. Lord, help me to walk in humility, speak with wisdom, and treat others with the same grace and respect You show me. Let my life reflect Your glory in every interaction. In Jesus' name, Amen.

KINGLY CHALLENGE

This week, walk out the principle that **Respect is Royalty**:

- **Honor a woman in your life**: Speak a kind word based on her strength, not her appearance. Make her feel seen and valued.
- **Call or visit an elder**: Ask for one piece of wisdom they wish young men today understood. Listen—and apply it.
- **Honor authority**: Whether it's a teacher, coach, or community leader, show respect in tone and attitude—even if you disagree.
- **Respect yourself**: Make one decision each day that aligns with your future as a man of God. Say no to peer pressure, trash talk, or toxic influence.
- **Speak like a king**: For 7 days, eliminate sarcasm, insults, or negativity from your words. Replace it with encouragement and truth.

- **Remember:** The way you treat others reflects the royalty within you. You are a king in training—so lead with honor.

King In Training: Godly Wisdom For My Younger Self

CHAPTER 6:

BROTHERS AND BATTLES

CHOOSING WISE FRIENDSHIPS, EMBRACING ACCOUNTABILITY, AND FIGHTING TEMPTATION

No king fights alone. Every king needs brothers he can trust—men who sharpen, protect, and challenge him to stay on the path of righteousness. The battles you face as a young man— temptation, peer pressure, identity struggles—can't always be won in isolation. That's why it matters who you walk with.

Growing up, I discovered just how powerful godly friendships can be. When I started building relationships with young men who loved God, worked hard, and wanted to grow, everything about me leveled up—my character, my mindset, and my destiny. The right friends can help you stay grounded when life tries to knock you off course.

Proverbs 13:20 (NIV) says, *"Walk with the wise and become wise, for a companion of fools suffers harm."* That one verse can protect your entire future. It doesn't say you *might* suffer, it says you *will*. Whoever you choose to walk with will either bring you wisdom or bring you wounds.

Wise friendships are built on truth, trust, and transparency. These aren't "yes men" who agree with everything you say. These are brothers who love you enough to call you out when you're slipping. The kind of men who will pull you to the side and say, "That's not who you are." You don't need a crowd, you need a few committed friends who want to see you win spiritually, mentally, and morally.

Accountability is not a weakness, it's a weapon. When you're truly accountable, you're inviting someone into your life to help you stay aligned with your values and your faith. Kings are not just held accountable by others, they *embrace* accountability. Why? Because they know the enemy is subtle. Temptation doesn't always come in loud and obvious ways. Sometimes it shows up in silence—in the form of secret habits, quiet compromises, and private decisions.

That's why every king needs to be honest about the battles he faces. Whether it's lust, pride, laziness, addiction, or anger—real strength begins with real confession. God doesn't expect perfection, but He does call us to purity. The only way to win the battle over sin is to stop pretending you're not in a fight.

James 5:16 (ESV) says, *"Therefore, confess your sins to one another and pray for one another, that you may be healed. The prayer of a righteous person has great power as it is working."* There is healing in confession. There is power in brotherhood. When you hide your struggles, you feed your shame. But when you bring your struggle into the light, the darkness loses its grip.

You are not weak because you're tempted. Jesus Himself was tempted. You're weak when you think you can handle it all by yourself.

That's where many young men fall. They confuse secrecy with strength. But kings-in-training understand that surrender to God is the key to victory.

Sometimes the strongest thing you can say is, "I need help."
There have been seasons in my life where I had to be brutally honest with a mentor or a brother in Christ. I had to say, "Hey, I'm struggling with this." And instead of judging me, they stood with me. They reminded me of who I was, prayed with me, and helped me fight through it. That's what real brotherhood looks like.
It's not about gossip. It's about growth.

So, who are your brothers in battle? Who do you call when you're tempted to give in? Who checks on your walk with God—not just your social media followers or your game stats? Surround yourself with men who will fight with you and for you. Build a tribe of warriors who remind you that holiness is possible and that kings don't quit.

Reflection Questions

1. What do wise friendships look like in your life right now?
2. Have you ever had a friend hold you accountable for a decision? How did it feel?
3. What temptations do you find hardest to resist, and who helps you stand strong?
4. Why is it important to choose friends who share your values and goals?
5. What kind of brother or friend do you want to be to others?

Personal Prayer

Lord, I thank You for the gift of brotherhood and accountability. Help me to choose friends who honor You and give me the courage to be transparent about my battles. Teach me to value wisdom over popularity, and purity over pride. Strengthen me in moments of temptation and give me the humility to seek help when I'm weak. Surround me with godly brothers who will walk with me, pray for me, and sharpen me for my calling. In Jesus' name, Amen.

Kingly Challenge

- **Evaluate your circle**: Write down the names of your five closest friends. Are they helping you grow or pulling you away from God's purpose for your life?
- **Reach out to an accountability partner**: Choose someone you trust—a mentor, youth leader, or spiritual brother—and commit to checking in weekly about your spiritual walk.
- **Be honest with one struggle**: Confess a temptation you've been battling to someone safe and godly. Let them pray with you and hold you up.
- **Limit isolation**: For the next 7 days, don't let a day go by without connecting with a godly influence—whether it's a conversation, prayer, or time in the Word together.
- **Choose one godly friendship to strengthen**: Call or meet up with a brother in Christ and tell him how much

you appreciate his walk and witness. Encourage each other.
- **Remember:** The battles you face aren't meant to be fought alone. A king is only as strong as the brothers who stand beside him.

Robert P. Harris, Jr.

Chapter 7:

Legacy Over Hype

LIVING FOR ETERNAL IMPACT, NOT TEMPORARY APPLAUSE—BECOMING A MAN OTHERS CAN FOLLOW

There's a big difference between hype and legacy. Hype is loud, fast, and attention-grabbing. It's all about how many people are watching, how many likes you can get, and how viral you can go. But legacy? Legacy is quiet, steady, and powerful. It's not about who claps for you in the moment, it's about who walks in your footsteps after you're gone.

As a young man, it's easy to fall into the trap of living for applause. We want people to notice our gifts, admire our talent, and praise our accomplishments. But kings-in-training must rise above that mindset. We're not called to impress the world—we're called to influence it for God.

Proverbs 22:1 (NIV) says, *"A good name is more desirable than great riches; to be esteemed is better than silver or gold."* That's a legacy. A good name. A reputation built on character, consistency, and Christ. Not how many followers you have, but how many people trust your word. Not how loud your voice is online, but how strong your walk is in private.

Legacy doesn't just happen. You build it—brick by brick—through your daily choices. Every time you tell the truth when lying would be easier, every time you walk away from temptation, every time you serve when you could have been selfish—you're building a foundation others can stand on. And that matters more than anything hype could ever offer.

The hype dies down. Fame fades. Trends change. But the impact you make through godly living? That lasts.

I think of the men who impacted my life. They weren't perfect. They didn't have big platforms. But they were solid. Consistent. Respectful. God-fearing. The way they carried themselves taught me how to walk with dignity. The way they handled pressure taught me how to lead with integrity. They weren't chasing fame—they were leaving footprints.

Matthew 5:16 (NIV) reminds us, *"Let your light shine before others, that they may see your good deeds and glorify your Father in heaven."* That's what legacy does. It shines in such a way that people don't just praise you—they see God.

Legacy isn't always public. Sometimes it's found in private sacrifice, praying for your future family, choosing purity over popularity, helping someone without posting about it. It's about how you live when no one's clapping. When you're no longer chasing validation, you're free to walk in purpose.

Living for legacy means you stop asking, "What can I get right now?" and start asking, "What am I building for the future?" It changes your goals. You stop living for Friday night and start living for the next generation. You stop chasing recognition and start becoming the kind of man others want to follow.

When you choose legacy over hype, you become a bridge between where people are and where God is calling them. You become a leader. Not just someone with a title, but someone with truth. Someone whose presence brings peace. Someone whose life points to Jesus.

But here's the challenge—legacy building takes time. It requires patience and maturity. It means saying "no" to shortcuts and quick applause. It means walking the narrow road when everyone else is chasing the spotlight. But I promise you this: God honors those who walk humbly and faithfully before Him.

Galatians 6:9 (NIV) encourages us, *"Let us not become weary in doing good, for at the proper time we will reap a harvest if we do not give up."* The seeds you sow today in obedience, character, and faithfulness will become the fruit others eat tomorrow.

So, will you settle for hype, or will you live for legacy?

REFLECTION QUESTIONS

1. What does the word 'legacy' mean to you?
2. Are you living more for eternal impact or for temporary applause? Why?
3. Who in your life is a model of legacy living?
4. What values do you want people to remember you for?
5. How can you start building a God-honoring legacy today?

Personal Prayer

Heavenly Father, help me to live for more than applause. Teach me to value eternal impact over temporary attention. Show me how to walk with humility, integrity, and purpose. Let my life be a reflection of Your goodness and love. I don't want to chase trends—I want to build truth. I want to leave behind more than memories—I want to leave a legacy. Guide me daily as I grow into the man You've called me to be. In Jesus' name, Amen.

KINGLY CHALLENGE

- **Write your future legacy statement**: Take 5–10 minutes and write how you want to be remembered. What kind of man, son, friend, or father, do you want to be?
- **Choose purpose over popularity**: This week, turn down one thing that boosts your image but distracts you from your purpose.
- **Honor a legacy builder in your life**: Reach out to a mentor, elder, or leader who has made an impact on your life and thank them.
- **Sow a legacy seed**: Do one act of quiet service this week that no one sees but God. Journal how it made you feel.
- **Start building now**: Identify one habit you need to break and one habit you need to start to build the legacy God has called you to.
- **Remember:** Hype fades, but legacy speaks long after you're gone. You're not just living for today—you're building for

eternity. Live like a king whose name will be remembered in heaven.

King In Training: Godly Wisdom For My Younger Self

CHAPTER 8:

THE MIRROR OF A KING

*SEEING YOURSELF THROUGH GOD'S EYES—
RESTORING CONFIDENCE, IDENTITY, AND
PURPOSE AS A MAN OF GOD*

A mirror can reveal only what stands in front of it—but God's mirror shows the man you are becoming. When you stare into the world's mirror, you see height, grades, speed, social status, or whatever people applaud. When you stare into God's mirror, you see destiny — a chosen man, fearfully and wonderfully made, empowered for Kingdom purpose. The journey from self-doubt to God-confidence begins when you trade the first mirror for the second.

1. Gideon: From Hiding to Hero

Gideon's story is every insecure man's story. He started in a winepress, hiding grains from the Midianite army and hiding himself from inner fear. Yet God greeted him with a title that sounded absurd: **"The LORD is with you, mighty warrior!"** (Judges 6:12). Gideon's first response wasn't courage; it was complaint: *"My clan is the weakest... I am the least in my family."* God never argued with Gideon's résumé. He simply promised, **"I will be with you."**

God wasn't concerned with Gideon's status; He cared about Gideon's willingness. That truth rewrites every insecurity you carry: your Father is not scanning your report card, bank account, or highlight reel—He is searching for a heart that will say, "Yes, Lord."

2. THE WEIGHT OF SELF-DOUBT

I understand Gideon. Growing up, I questioned whether I was smart enough to keep up in class and athletic enough to earn respect on the field. Every mistake felt like proof that I didn't measure up. Self-doubt talks loudly:

- *"You're too small."*
- *"You're not gifted enough."*
- *"Someone else could do it better."*

If you allow those whispers to linger, they become labels. And labels can lock a king into a prison of mediocrity.

But here is the King's mirror: **Ephesians 2:10 (NIV)** says, *"For we are God's workmanship, created in Christ Jesus to do good works, which God prepared in advance for us to do."* Workmanship means "masterpiece." Before you earned a grade or scored a point, God stamped **masterpiece** over your life.

3. Trading Insecurity for Identity

How did Gideon move from hiding to leading 300 warriors? He embraced God's identity over his insecurity. The same steps apply to us:

1. **Hear the Call** – God calls you by your destiny, not your deficiency.
2. **Tear Down the Lies** – Gideon destroyed his father's idol altar at night (Judges 6:25-27). You must tear down mental idols too—false beliefs that say worth = popularity, appearance, or applause.
3. **Step in Obedience** – Gideon obeyed in small tasks first; confidence grows with every obedient step.

4. **Rely on God's Strength** – God reduced Gideon's army so no one could boast. Your confidence is safest when it rests on God, not ego.

4. From Self-Confidence to God-Confidence

Self-confidence relies on how well you perform; God-confidence relies on how faithful He is. When my mind spiraled—*"You're not smart enough,"*—God answered with **James 1:5**: *"If any of you lacks wisdom, you should ask God… and it will be given to you."* When I wondered if I was athletic enough, He reminded me of **Philippians 4:13**: *"I can do all things through Christ who strengthens me."*

God-confidence doesn't deny weaknesses; it invites God into them. A king's power is not perfection—it is partnership with the Perfect One.

5. Practical Ways to See What God Sees

Mirror Swap	World's Mirror	King's Mirror
Source of Worth	Performance & popularity	Identity in Christ (Gal. 3:26)
Definition of Strength	Physical dominance	Spiritual dependence (2 Cor. 12:9)
Future Outlook	Fear of failure	Faith in purpose (Jer. 29:11)

1. **Daily Scripture Affirmations** – Speak verses that declare who you are: chosen, forgiven, empowered.
2. **Gratitude Journal** – List three ways God used you each day; trains your eyes to see impact over inadequacy.
3. **Serve Others Quietly** – Nothing silences insecurity like lifting someone else; service shifts focus from what you lack to what you carry.
4. **Mentor Feedback** – Invite a trusted leader to speak into blind spots and

strengths, outside perspective polishes self-perception.

Reflection Questions

1. What do you see when you look in the mirror—physically, emotionally, and spiritually?
2. How has self-doubt ever held you back from walking in your calling?
3. What can you learn from Gideon's story about confidence and purpose?
4. How does God see you, and how does that view differ from how you see yourself?
5. What are some steps you can take to build godly confidence and self-esteem?

PERSONAL PRAYER

Father, thank You for seeing a mighty warrior in me even when I feel unqualified. Replace every label of "not enough" with Your truth that I am Your masterpiece. Like Gideon, I choose willingness over status and faith over fear. Teach me to view myself through Heaven's mirror, to walk with humble confidence, and to fulfill the purpose You prepared for me. In Jesus' name, Amen.

KINGLY CHALLENGE

- **Mirror Verse** – Memorize Judges 6:12. Each morning, look in the mirror and declare, "The LORD is with me, mighty warrior!"
- **List & Replace** – Write three recurring self-doubts. Cross them out and write a matching scripture of truth beside each.
- **Serve Beyond Status** – This week, do one act of service that gains zero applause (help a neighbor, tutor a classmate, clean without being asked). Journal how God used you.
- **Courage Call** – Share a dream or calling you've been hiding with a trusted mentor or friend. Ask them to pray and hold you accountable for one next step.
- **Small-Step Obedience** – Choose one area you've avoided (academic challenge, fitness goal, spiritual discipline). Take a measurable action within 48 hours as your "winepress to warrior" moment.
- **Remember:** Kings aren't crowned by perfection but by permission—permission

for God to rewrite their reflection. Look in His mirror and rise.

King In Training: Godly Wisdom For My Younger Self

ABOUT THE AUTHOR

Robert P. Harris, Jr. was born in Shelby, Mississippi, and raised in a loving village of family members who helped shape and mold him into the man he is today. A proud graduate of Broadstreet High School, Robert continued his education and earned degrees from Coahoma Community College and the University of Arkansas at Pine Bluff. He later earned a certification in HVAC from ATI Technical School.

Robert is a Certified Life Coach in Male Mentorship and a dedicated mentor to men both young and old. He also serves as a youth football coach for the MYFL. His own journey through football—from high school to college—instilled in him powerful lessons about character, discipline, life skills, and work ethic.

Driven by a deep desire to see young men thrive, Robert is passionate about providing Godly training that empowers them to become the best versions of themselves, productive members of society, and faithful representatives of Jesus Christ.

Since 2005, Robert has been joyfully married to his devoted wife, Tiffany Harris. Together, they are the proud parents of their twin children, Robert I. Harris and Moriah E. Harris.

www.ingramcontent.com/pod-product-compliance
Lightning Source LLC
Chambersburg PA
CBHW050657160426
43194CB00010B/1973